GW00497029

The #2021 Air Fryer Cookbook

Quick and Delicious Air Fryer Recipes for the Whole Family incl. Tasty Desserts Special

Beth Gardner

Copyright © [2020] [Beth Gardner]

All rights reserved

All rights for this book here presented belong exclusively to the author.
Usage or reproduction of the text is forbidden and requires a clear consent of the
author in case of expectations.

ISBN- 9798684311161

Table of Contents

Introduction

Preparing healthy meals is an essential activity in every household around the world. Because of this, kitchenware manufacturers have been forced to come up with new cooking appliances that make this process easier. In fact, most modern cooking appliances have a feature or two that makes healthy meal preparation a reality. Indulging in deep-fried meals is a guilty pleasure that we simply can't stay away from thanks to the irresistible taste. However, the air fryer is here to take the guilt away as you relish on your meal of choice. This text will give you all the insights you need to know about the air fryer. With the help of our top recipes, be sure to prepare savory meals for you and yours. Watch out for our top 10 air fryer dessert recipe!

What is an Air Fryer?

If you are an avid cook, then you surely have heard about the air fryer, but do you know what it really is? An Air fryer essentially is a kitchen appliance that works similarly to the convection oven in the sense that it both roasts and bakes. The air fryer also mimics the cooking nature of the deep fryer but with little to no oil at all, impressive right!

Cooking mechanism of the Air Fryer

This cooking appliance is simply a miniature convection oven that cook food by the circulation of hot air around the food. The appliance has a high-speed fan that circulates hot air around the food, producing that nice crisp layer that we all crave for in deep-fried meals. Juxtaposed to the conventional deep frying mechanism, the air fryer uses hot air to prepare meals that would otherwise be prepared by immersion in hot oil. What this means for you is that you get to enjoy savory, crispy meals with little to no oil at all. To put context to this, the air fryer prepares and brown chicken, fish, potato chips, and even pastry with 80% less oil than the conventional deep fryer.

Why the Air Fryer not the Convection Oven

The air fryer works in the same way as the convection oven and that's a fact. But why should you have the former rather than the latter? To begin, the countertop is a contentious commodity that is just not enough no matter how big space you have. The air fryer is small and just the right size to fit into that small space on your counter. On the other hand, the convection oven is quite large and the smaller versions cannot be compared to the traditional one. Also, thanks to the small size, the air fryer circulates air faster and efficiently around the food allowing you to enjoy your meals in record time. One other additional feature is the basket which allows enough heat circulation at the bottom of your meals reducing the cooking time even more.

Difference between an Air Fryer and a Deep Fryer

The first and most evident difference is in the cooking mechanism. The air fryer cooks food at high temperatures with the help of high powered fans for even circulation of heat. The deep fryer on the other hand makes use of preheated oil to cook food. While both appliances cook food quickly, the air fryer is relatively quick because it requires no preheat time. Food usually turns out brown and crispy but don't always taste the same. Deep frying usually employs battered foods that cook differently on the air fryer and as a result, the food doesn't always taste the same. However, you could coat the butter with oil to get them nice and brown before cooking in the air fryer. Nonetheless, frying wet and flour-based batters is not this appliance's strong suit.

What size do you need?

There are different types and sizes of air fryers in the market. The most common type is the basket-type-air fryer that looks like a chunky coffee maker. While other types have multiple functions, this one is exclusive for air frying. Let us discuss more on this common basket-type air fryer.

It will be to your benefit to know and accept that you cannot prepare heavy batches of food in the air fryer. The smaller 1.75 to 3-quart fryer can only serve a maximum of two people with no significant leftovers. The larger 4-5 quart carriers or when you need to prepare large amounts of food, you will require to do so in batches. While this may seem like a drag, keep in mind that food doesn't take long on an air fryer.

Whether you are using the basket-type or any other air-fryer you will get invaluable insight from these tips.

First-time use

The first thing to do after getting your fryer is to unbox and disassemble all the removable parts which should include, the basket and grate. Wash these parts and dry before reassembling. Some brands will require running the appliance empty for some time to expel some gas and the initial chemical smell that almost all appliances have when new. Always run your appliance on a heat resistant surface and away from the wall.

Cleaning your Air Fryer

Cleaning is not usually the fan part for so many of us, however, understanding the right cleaning techniques and tweaks could lessen the load tremendously. Also, a good cleanup often increases the shelf life of most appliances. So how do we clean this sleek appliance?

Parts to wash after every use

The air fryer is made up of individual removable parts making cleanup effortless. To begin, the pan, basket, and the tray ought to be cleaned every time they are used. It will interest you to know that these parts can be cleaned with regular washing detergents and warm water. However, if you are not in the mood, you could toss them into the washer, these parts are usually dishwasher friendly. It is good practice to confirm with the respective manufacturer beforehand. Cleaning the interior is also quite easy, while it is not dishwasher friendly, a simple wipe using a damp cloth with some detergent should easily do the trick. Remember to dry each part individually before reassembling together.

Parts to wash occasionally

The air fryer uses little oil when cooking, therefore, the cooking process makes little mess altogether. In effect, expect little greasing on the outside part of the appliance after cooking, so you don't have to clean the exterior after every use. After a couple of uses, ensure the appliance is unplugged before wiping with a damp cloth with some detergent. It's that easy!

Often, remember to check on the heating coil, if you notice some grease stains, clean with a damp cloth.

Other cleaning and handling tips

If you notice some foul odor coming from the appliance, this means that some grease or food particle is trapped somewhere. There is a simple trick to address this, form a paste from baking soda and water and scrub the interior using an old toothbrush. The smell should be gone in the next use.

It is important to avoid scrubbing the interior of the appliance with metallic objects for instance spoons. This will easily compromise the nonstick coat rendering the appliance ineffective. Always remember to unplug and let the appliance cool down before any attempt to clean.

What to expect and remember

Cooks food fast

One of the many upsides to the fryer is about how food cooks in record time. Read the user manual for the temperatures for the most common foods. A rule of thumb, the lesser the food the faster it will cook.

It's ok to remove the basket for a quick peek

The appliance is made in such a way that it isn't a necessity to switch it off before drawing the basket. Once you draw the basket, it automatically switches off making it super safe to peek and shake the contents in the basket often. Ensure the drawer is all the way in when you are putting it back otherwise, the fryer won't turn back on.

The grate should always be in the bucket

Doing this will increase the efficiency of the appliance by ensuring proper circulation of the hot air and also makes sure the food doesn't sit on excess oil.

Air Fryers are quite loud

You should expect a considerable amount of noise from the fan when the appliance is working. No worries, you won't have to tolerate it for long since once again, food cooks quite fast.

Common things to observe when using an Air Fryer

Watch the amount of oil

Go easy on the oil. Too much oil only means that it will collect on the drawer under the grate or may smoke in extreme cases. So if there is already some fat on the food, there is no need for any addition. In essence, fatty foods do not require any oil addition while vegetables benefit heavily from oil coating for that nice brown finish. So the amount of oil used is entirely dependent on the food you intend to prepare.

Watch out on the type of oil

Do not use low smoke point oils for preparing meals on the air fryer. Remember, air fryers get really hot and low smoke point oils, for instance, olive oil smokes easy and gets a bad aftertaste. Some of the oils you could use are canola oil, vegetable oil, and also peanut oil which have relatively higher smoke points.

Forget greasing the drawer with oil

The basket is made of nonstick finish that should not be greased under any circumstance. The reason being that over time the grease will compromise the nonstick coat and cause damages along the line. So instead of greasing the basket, why not toss your food in oil before cooking. It's a much better idea! Some recipes might recommend spraying; you could do this occasionally.

Always shake the basket

Most recipes will recommend a periodic shake of the basket within the cooking period. This is very important because it encourages proper exposure of the food to the heat and in the end achieving that elusive perfect turnout. However, if you fail to do so, it's not the end of the world but your food won't turn out as perfect as you would want. When preparing large chunks of food, flip instead of shaking.

Avoid putting the drawer on the countertop

If you don't place the pan directly from the cooktop onto the counter, then you shouldn't do that with the drawer either. After cooking, the bottom of the drawer is the hottest and may damage your countertop. What you do is to remove from the fryer and place it on an already set potholder.

Don't crowd the drawer

Air fryers have little space to work with, so watch out and do not overload the drawer. To get restaurant-quality browning, don't overcrowd the drawer. While there is no specific marker for when the drawer is full, you will just know when there are enough potato chips in there. You will eventually realize that food cooks faster and nicer when they are less crowded in the fryer.

Handle the Fryer with caution

Once the fryer is running, do not assume that the entire exterior is uniformly cold. The fryer might not get red hot but it gets hot enough to burn your hand especially around the back. To be safe only grab the drawer by the handle whenever you want to peek or when you want to remove it altogether.

Empty the drawer with caution

Once you are done cooking, do not just throw caution to the wind and pour everything into a bowl. Remember, excess oils drain and collects on the drawer which may lead to greasy food, cause a mess all over your countertop or worse, spill, and burn you. It is a good idea to use tongs to grab a piece. After the other till you empty the drawer.

Recipes

BREAKFAST

AIR FRYER DONUTS

Time: 15 minutes | Serves 8

Kcal 316, Carbs 42g/1.48oz, Fats 15g/0.53oz, Proteins 3g/0.12oz, Fiber 1g/0.03oz

INGREDIENTS

- 450g/16oz of refrigerated flaky jumbo biscuits
- Coconut/olive oil spray
- 8g/2 teaspoon of ground cinnamon
- 64g/½ a cup of granulated sugar
- 60ml/4 teaspoons of melted butter

PREPARATION

1. Combine and mix in a bowl before setting aside.
2. Unravel the biscuits from the box, place them on a firm surface and make circular 1-inch holes in each biscuit.
3. Brush some coconut/ olive oil on the basket (go easy on the oil). Stay clear of nonstick oils, they could damage the basket coat.
4. Put 4 donuts at a time on the air fryer. Separate them completely they should not be touching.
5. Air fry the donuts under a temperature of 176°C/350°F until nice and brown.
6. Coat with cinnamon sugar once they are done before serving.
7. Don't forget to enjoy it!

LOW CARB BREAKFAST CASSEROLE

Time: 25 minutes | Serves 8

Kcal 282, Carbs 682mg/0.02oz, Fats 23g/0.81oz, Proteins 15g/0.53oz, Fiber 0g

INGREDIENTS

- 450g/1lb of ground sausage
- 2g/½ a teaspoon of garlic sauce
- 4g/1 teaspoon of fennel seeds
- 8 whole eggs
- 32g/¼ a cup of diced onions
- A single diced green bell pepper
- 32g/½ a cup of shredded Colby jack cheese

PREPARATION

1. Using a skillet, brown the sausages for a few minutes.
2. Put in the pepper and onions to the ground sausages and cook some more till the veggies are nice and cooked.
3. Spray the air fryer pan lightly with some nonstick coat oil and put the sausage onion mixture on the pan.
4. Add some cheese then gently add in the eggs.
5. Finish off with some fennel seeds and garlic salt over the eggs.
6. Put the pan directly into the air fryer then bake for 15 minutes over a temperature of 390°C/298°F.
7. Remove, serve, and enjoy!

AIR FRYER BREAKFAST SAUSAGES

Time: 20 minutes | Servings 8
Kcal 219, Carbs 9g/0.3oz, Protein 14g/0.5oz, Fats 12g/0.4oz, Fiber 1g/0.03oz

INGREDIENTS

- 8g/2 teaspoons of fennel seeds
- 4g/1 teaspoon of sea salt
- 450g/1lb of ground pork
- 8g/2 teaspoons of garlic powder
- 450g/1lb of ground turkey
- 8g/2 teaspoons of rubbed sage
- 4g/1 teaspoon of paprika
- 5ml/1 tablespoon of maple syrup
- 4g/1 teaspoon of dried thyme

PREPARATION

1. In a large pan, combine and mix the pork and turkey.
2. Combine and mix the remaining ingredients thoroughly in a separate bowl.
3. Pour the spice mixture into the meat and mix using your hands making sure everything is nice and coated.
4. Scoop spoonfuls of the seasoned meat and form patties using your hands before placing in the air fryer.
5. You will need to do this in two batches to achieve an even and proper finish.
6. Set the temperatures to 187°C/370°F before cooking for 10 minutes.
7. Do the same for the remaining patties and serve.

AIR FRYER BREAKFAST POCKETS

Time: 15 minutes | Servings 2
Kcal 392, Fat 20g/0.71oz, Carbs 8g/0.28oz, Fiber 6g/0.09oz, Protein 18g/0.63oz

INGREDIENTS

- 5 full eggs
- A box of puff pastry sheets
- 32g/½ a cup of shredded cheddar cheese
- 32g/½ a cup of cooked sausage crumbles
- 32g/½ a cup of cooked bacon.

PREPARATION

1. Crack and whisk the eggs in a bowl.
2. Scramble the eggs on a skillet then introduce the meat to the egg mixture while cooking.
3. On a chopping board, spread out the pastry and cut into rectangles using a knife or a cookie cutter.
4. Top the cooked egg meat mixture onto half of the pastry rectangles.
5. Place another pastry triangle to seal in the egg and meat combo.
6. If you desire, spray some oil on the pockets to achieve a smooth oily finish.
7. Cook the pockets for 10 minutes in the fryer at 187°C/370°F.
8. Keep a close eye on them and toss frequently for even cooking.

BACON AND EGG BREAKFAST BISCUIT BOMBS

Time: 55 minutes | Servings 8
Kcal 220, Carbs 17g/0.6oz, Fats 12g/0.42oz, Proteins 7g/0.24oz, Fiber 0g

INGREDIENTS

- 17g/1 tablespoon of butter
- 60g/2oz of sharp cheddar cheese
- 3 beaten eggs
- 4 pieces of bacon sliced into ½ inches
- 1g/¼ teaspoon of cheese
- 10oz can of buttermilk biscuits
- 10ml/2 tablespoons of water

PREPARATION

1. Prepare two 8-inch round parchment paper coating them with oil and line the basket bottom nicely.
2. Sauté the bacon on a pan over high heat till crispy before removing from the pan.
3. Melt butter on the same pan and add two beaten eggs and cook till thick but still moist.
4. Remove from heat before adding in the bacon and allow cooling for 5 minutes.
5. Separate the dough into 5 biscuits.
6. Make two layers out of each biscuit and press each layer to a 4-inch thin round dough.
7. Scoop a spoonful of the egg and bacon mixture into each round and sprinkle some cheese on top before folding nicely into a sealed circular ball.
8. Make an egg wash out of the remaining egg and water and brush each bomb with the wash.
9. Place 5 bombs on the pre-oiled parchment paper and cook for 8 minutes under 162°C/325°F.
10. You will need to toss around frequently during the cooking process.
11. Serve while warm and eat with a hot beverage of your choice.

AIR FRYER BREAKFAST POTATOES

Time 20 minutes | Servings 3

Kcal 375, Carbs 67g/2.3oz, Fats 7g/0.25oz, Proteins 13g/0.03oz, Fiber 13g/0.03oz

INGREDIENTS

- 1 chopped green bell pepper
- 15ml/1 tablespoon of olive oil
- 1g/¼ teaspoon of pepper
- 680g/1½lb of potatoes
- ¼ chopped onion
- 2g/½ a tablespoon of paprika
- A pinch of salt

PREPARATION

1. Carefully, wash the bell peppers and potatoes.
2. Now dice the potatoes before soaking in water and allow them to stay for 30 minutes before pat drying.
3. Chop the bell peppers, onion, and potatoes into smaller pieces.
4. Mince the garlic if you haven't already.
5. Combine all the ingredients and mix thoroughly before emptying into the air fryer basket.
6. Bake the eggs in the air fryer on 200°C/392°F for 25 minutes tossing after every 10 minutes to achieve an even finish.
7. Serve when ready.

AIR FRYER BREAKFAST EGG ROLLS

Time: 25 minutes | Serves 3

Kcal 78, Carbs 7g/0.23oz, Fats 6g/0.06oz, Proteins 3g/0.09oz, Fiber 1g/0.03oz

INGREDIENTS

- 4g/1 teaspoon of pepper
- 32g/½ a cup of shredded cheddar cheese
- 15ml/1 tablespoon of olive oil
- A pinch of salt
- 2 whole eggs
- 30ml/2 tablespoons of milk
- Water
- 6 egg roll wrappers
- 2 sausage patties

PREPARATION

1. In a skillet, cook the sausages according to package instructions. Once cooked, chop into smaller chunks.

2. Combine the beaten eggs, milk, pepper and a pinch of salt then mix.

3. Add some oil to a pan and heat up over medium heat.

4. Empty the egg mixture into the preheated oil and cook for some minutes till you achieve scrambled eggs.

5. Put in the sausages and cook for some more.

6. Place the egg roll wrapper on a hard surface and create a diamond shape before topping with the egg sausage mixture.

7. Fold the bottom part of the wrapper up and over the mixture tightly and neatly. Now fold the sides creating an envelope shape opening. Finally, wrap the top around the wrapper and seal by brushing some water along the edges.

8. Preheat the air fryer to a temperature of 200°C/392°F for 5 minutes.

9. Lightly, brush the wrappers with oil and carefully place them on the basket and allow cooking for 8 minutes.

10. Toss and turn the rolls after 4 minutes and cook for an additional 4 minutes.

11. Enjoy!

AIR FRYER FRENCH TOAST STICKS

Time: 17 minutes | Servings 2
Kcal 178, Carbs 2g/0.07oz, Fats 15g/0.53oz, Proteins 5g/0.18oz, Fiber 0g

INGREDIENTS

- A pinch of salt
- A pinch of ground salt
- 4g/1 teaspoon of maple syrup
- 4 pieces of bread
- 34g/2 teaspoon of butter
- 4g/1 teaspoon of nutmeg
- 2 beaten eggs
- A pinch of ground cloves
- 4g/1 teaspoon of ground cinnamon

PREPARATION

1. Bring the air fryer to a temperature of 180°C/356°F.
2. Mix 2 beaten eggs, a pinch of nutmeg, ground cloves, salt, and cinnamon then mix thoroughly.
3. Apply some butter on both sides of the bread pieces before slicing them into strips.
4. Insert each bread piece in the egg mixture and allow it to soak up before placing it in the air fryer.
5. Cook for 2 minutes before removing the pan and spraying the bread with some cooking spray.
6. Once coated evenly, return the pan in the fryer and cook for an additional 4 minutes checking frequently to ensure even cooking.
7. Remove from the air fryer once the egg cooks and bread pieces are nice and brown.
8. Sprinkle some icing sugar on top and some maple syrup to your liking.

AIR FRYER BAKED EGG CUPS WITH SPINACH & CHEESE

Time: 15 minutes | Serves 1

Kcal 115, Carbs 1g/0.03oz, Fats 7g/0.24oz, Proteins 10g/0.35oz, Fiber 0g

INGREDIENTS

- A pinch of salt
- 1 large egg
- 15ml/1 tablespoon of milk
- 4g/1 teaspoon of ground black pepper
- 15ml/1 tablespoon of frozen spinach
- 10ml/2 teaspoons of grated cheese

PREPARATION

1. Gently spray the insides of the muffin cups with some oil.
2. Crack an egg into the muffin cup and add milk, cheese, and spinach.
3. Add some pepper and salt on the egg white to taste and stir gently not to break the yolk.
4. Air fry for 6 minutes. Remember if you are cooking more than one cup, you should give some more time. A single cup takes roughly 6 minutes in the air fryer. When cooking in a ceramic ramekin, expect the muffins to cook for longer.
5. Frequently check on the eggs to ensure the yolks cook to your desired texture.

AIR FRIED CRISPY BACON

Time: 10 minutes | Serves 1
Kcal 177, Carbs 1g/0.03oz, Fats 13g/0.46oz, Proteins 13g/0.46oz, Fiber 0g

INGREDIENTS

- 450g/1lb of bacon

PREPARATION

1. Put the bacon in the basket. Cook in more than one batch relative to the size of the fryer.
2. Air fry for 5 minutes under a temperature of 176°C/350°F.
3. Check on the bacon after 5 minutes lapses then flip to the other side and cook further for about 5 minutes or till you achieve your preferred crispiness.
4. Once cooked, use tongs to remove and place on a serving plate with paper towels.
5. Allow cooling before serving.
6. Enjoy with a sauce of your choice.

AIR FRYER APPLE FRITTERS

Time: 25 minutes | Serves 4
Kcal 296, Carbs 64.9g/2.26oz, Fats 2.1g/0.08oz,
Proteins 5.5g/ 0.19oz, Fiber 1.9g/0.06oz

INGREDIENTS

- Pam butter cooking spray
- 1 whole egg
- 128g/1 cup wheat flour
- 6g/1½ teaspoon of leavening agents
- 65ml/¼ a cup of milk
- 32g/¼ cup of sugar
- 34g/2 tablespoons of granulated sugar
- An apple
- A pinch of table salt
- 2g/½ teaspoon of cinnamon
- 2½ml/½ teaspoon of vanilla extract

PREPARATION

1. Bring the air fryer to a temperature of 176°C/350°F.
2. Carefully line the basket with pre-oiled parchment paper.
3. Combine and mix flour, salt, milk, baking powder, eggs, and ¼ cup of sugar in a medium bowl and stir till even.
4. In a separate bowl, mix cinnamon and 2 tablespoons of salt. Drizzle on the diced apples and coat evenly.
5. Give the apples an even coat of the flour mixture.
6. Put the apple fritters into the basket then fry for about 5 minutes before flipping and cooking for an additional 5 minutes.
7. Combine and mix the vanilla extract, some milk and confectioner's sugar till even. Glaze the fritters with the vanilla mixture and allow cooking.

AIR FRYER OMELET

Time: 8 minutes | Servings 1

Kcal 133, Fats 1g/0.03oz, Carbs 2g/0.07oz, Fiber 1g/0.03oz, Protein 9g/0.11oz

INGREDIENTS

- 2 eggs
- A pinch of salt
- 32g/¼ cup of shredded cheese
- 64ml/¼ cup of milk
- 4g/1 teaspoon of breakfast seasoning.
- Meat and veggies (ham, green onions, red bell peppers, and mushrooms) diced

PREPARATION

1. Crack the eggs in a bowl and whisk thoroughly with the milk.
2. Season the egg mixture with a pinch of salt.
3. Put all the ham and veggies to the egg mixture.
4. Grease a pan with some oil before pouring in the egg mixtures.
5. Now put the pan into the basket and let it cook for 8 minutes under a temperature of 176°C/350°F.
6. Top with some breakfast seasoning and cheese halfway through and allow them to finish off.
7. Transfer to a flat plate and garnish with the green onions.

MAIN COURSE RECIPES

AIR FRYER AVOCADO WEDGES WITH GARLIC AIOLI DIPPING SAUCE

Time 10 minutes | Servings 4
Kcal 281, Carbs 2g/0.07oz, Fats 29g/1oz, Protein 4g/0.14oz, Fiber4g/0.14oz

INGREDIENTS

- 2 large beaten eggs
- 2 avocados sliced into 4 equal wedges
- 96g/¾ cup of panko crumbs
- 64g/½ cup of all-purpose flour
- 6g/1½ teaspoons of garlic pepper
- 3 cloves of crushed garlic
- 250ml/1 cup of light mayonnaise
- A pinch of salt
- 2½ml/½ teaspoon of freshly squeezed lemon juice.

PREPARATION

1. Put garlic pepper and flour in the same bowl and mix.
2. Beat the eggs in a separate dish and whisk.
3. Put all the panko crumbs in another dish.
4. Coat each avocado wedge in the flour mixture, through the eggs, and finally coat evenly with the panko crumbs.
5. Gently spray nonstick cooking fat on the basket.
6. Carefully arrange the wedges on the basket ensuring there is space between each wedge before spraying with the nonstick oil.
7. Cook for 8 minutes at a temperature of 204°C/400°F tossing halfway through the cooking.
8. Mix and whisk together the mayo, salt, lemon juice, and garlic in a bowl till nice and even.
9. Serve the avocado with some garlic sauce on the side.

AIR FRYER TOFU

Time: 23 minutes | Serving 4

Kcal 94, Carbs 5g/0.18oz, Fats 6g/0.21oz, Proteins 5g/0.18oz, Fiber 0g

INGREDIENTS

- 15ml/1 tablespoon of avocado oil
- 4g/1 teaspoon of garlic powder
- A pinch of salt
- 2g/½ a teaspoon of black pepper
- 4g/1 teaspoon of paprika
- 8g/2 teaspoons of cornstarch
- 4g/1 teaspoon of onion powder
- 340g/12oz extra firm tofu

PREPARATION

1. Press the tofu sandwiched between two paper towels and plates. Preferably press with a heavy object like a 1kg/35oz can for 30 minutes.
2. Bring the air fryer to a temperature of 200°C/ 390°F.
3. Chop the pressed tofu down to ½ an inch cubes.
4. Let the tofu cubes coat in the avocado oil and coat evenly with the cornstarch.
5. Cover the tofu in the remaining spices and place them in the basket. Cook in two batched depending on the amount of tofu and size of the fryer.
6. Air fry for 13 minutes, tossing and shaking every 5 minutes till you achieve your desired finish.
7. You will know when the tofu is ready when the exterior hardens.
8. Serve and enjoy!

AIR FRYER CHICKEN BITES

Time: 40 minutes | Servings 4

Kcal 256, Carbs 14g/0.49oz, Fats 7g/0.27oz, Proteins 32g/1.13oz, Fiber 1g/0.03oz

INGREDIENTS

- 2 beaten eggs
- 4g/1 teaspoon of salt
- 2g/½ teaspoon of garlic powder
- 16g/¼ cup of panko breadcrumbs
- 16g/¼ cup of parmesan cheese
- 2g/½ teaspoon of onion powder
- 16g/¼ cup of whole wheat flour
- 450g/1lb of skinless boneless chicken breast
- 16g/¼ cup of breadcrumbs

PREPARATION

1. Slice the chicken breasts into 2-inch pieces.
2. Put the beaten eggs in a single bowl.
3. In another bowl, add in the whole wheat flour.
4. Combine the garlic powder, onion powder, salt, parmesan cheese, and the two breadcrumbs and mix well.
5. Use tongs to dip the chicken breast pieces in the three different bowls beginning with the flour and ending with the breadcrumb mix. Do this with all the chicken pieces.
6. Bring the air fryer to a temperature of 200°C/390°F and cook the chicken breasts in batches for **4** minutes per batch before flipping. Air fry for an additional 3 minutes until cooked through.
7. Serve with your desired dipping sauce.

CRISPY AIR FRYER BONE-IN CHICKEN THIGHS

Time: 40 minutes | Servings 4
Kcal 140, Carbs 1g/0.030z, Fats 5g/0.17oz, Proteins 22g/0.77oz, Fiber 1g/0.03oz

INGREDIENTS

- Oil spray
- 4 bone-in and skin-on chicken thighs
- 2g/½ teaspoon of thyme leaves
- 4g/1 teaspoon of onion powder
- A pinch of salt
- 2g/½ a teaspoon of paprika powder
- 4g/1 teaspoon of garlic powder
- 2g/½ a teaspoon of pepper

PREPARATION

1. Spray the chicken thighs with the oil on a plate.
2. Combine and mix all the spices and sprinkle all over each piece before carefully massaging with your hands.
3. Bring the air fryer to a temperature of 200°C/ 390°F.
4. Arrange all (only place two if you have a smaller version) and spread them out well the allow cooking for 15 minutes.
5. Flip each piece and allow cooking for an additional 10 minutes or until you get an internal temperature of 85°C/185°F.
6. Once cooked, allow the chicken pieces to cook for 5 minutes then serve.

AIR FRYER CAULIFLOWER CHICKPEA TACOS

Time: 30 minutes | Servings 4
Kcal 508, Carbs 77g/2.17oz, Fats 15g/0.53oz,
Proteins 20g/0.72oz, Fiber 16g/0.56oz

INGREDIENTS

- 30ml/2 tablespoons of olive oil
- 500g/4 cups of sliced cauliflower florets
- 566g/20oz can of rinsed and drained chicken peas
- 30ml/2 tablespoons of taco seasoning
- Coconut yogurt
- 500g/2 cups of shredded cabbage
- 8 small tortillas
- 2 sliced avocados

PREPARATION

1. Bring the air fryer to a temperature of 200°C/390°F.
2. Combine the shredded cauliflower and chicken peas in a large bowl before adding some taco seasoning and olive oil.
3. Now put the mixture in the basket and allow cooking for 20 minutes. Remember to shake the basket occasionally until cooked.
4. You will know the cauliflower is nice and ready when they turn to a brown color.
5. Remove from the basket when ready and serve in each taco the cauliflower, some avocado pieces, and drizzle the coconut yogurt.

AIR FRYER THAI SALMON PATTIES

Time: 25 minutes | Servings 4

Kcal 108, Carbs 6g/0.21oz, Fats 6g/0.21oz, Proteins 12g/0.42oz, Fiber 1g/0.03oz

INGREDIENTS

- 400g/14oz of canned salmon
- Spray oil
- Zest from 1 lime
- 2 whole eggs
- A pinch of salt
- 25g/1½ tablespoons of brown sugar
- 64g/½ a cup of panko breadcrumbs
- 25ml/1½ tablespoons of Thai red curry paste

PREPARATION

1. Mix up every ingredient thoroughly in a bowl.
2. Put in the salmon pieces and make sure they are well distributed through the mixture.
3. Now using your hands or any handy device, form patties 1-inch-thick and 3 inches across.
4. Bring the air fryer to a temperature of 180°C/360°F.
5. Spray both sides of the patties with oil. (Be careful not to overdo it.)
6. Cook the patties in batches relative to the size of the fryer. Cook for 4 minutes before flipping the other side and cooking for an additional 4 minutes.
7. Do the same for the rest of the patties till they are all cooked.

AIR FRYER SHRIMP

Time: 30 minutes | Servings 4

Kcal 187, Carbs 7g/0.24oz, Fats 7g/0.24oz, Proteins 23g/0.81oz, Fiber 2g/0.07oz

INGREDIENTS

- A pinch of salt
- 450g/1lb of raw shrimp
- 25ml/1½ tablespoons of olive oil
- 2 cloves of minced garlic
- 25ml/1½ tablespoons of lime juice
- Cilantro
- 25ml/1½ tablespoons of honey
- Lime wedges

PREPARATION

1. Mix lime juice, salt, garlic, olive oil, and honey in a bowl then stir together till you achieve an even consistency.
2. Put in the shrimp and allow them to sit and marinate for 30 minutes.
3. Bring the air fryer to a temperature of 200°C/390°F.
4. Shake to drain off excess marinade before arranging the entire batch of shrimp into the basket.
5. Air fry for 5 minutes shaking the shrimp halfway through. (You can cook for longer until nice and pink). Ensure the shrimp cooks through.
6. Remove from the fryer once ready and serve with some cilantro and lime wedges on the side.

BUFFALO WINGS WITH BLUE CHEESE DIP

Time: 30 minutes | Servings 4
Kcal 204, Fats 16g/0.6oz, Saturates 3g/0.1oz, Carbs 7g/0.25oz,
Sugar 0g, Fiber 3g/0.1oz, Protein 9g/0.32oz, Salt 0.27g/0.01oz

INGREDIENTS

- 4g/1 teaspoon of garlic powder
- 90ml/6 tablespoons of red hot sauce
- 740ml/6oz of 12-piece chicken wings
- 45ml/3 tablespoons of white vinegar
- 2g/½ teaspoon of kosher salt
- 4g/1 teaspoon of dried oregano
- 85ml/⅔ cup of Greek yogurt
- 10ml/½ a tablespoon of lemon juice
- 32g/¼ a cup of crumbled blue cheese
- 2 medium chopped carrots
- 2 chopped celery

PREPARATION

1. Put oregano, hot sauce, vinegar, garlic powder, and some salt in a bowl and mix well. Add in the chicken wings and ensure each piece is nice and coated.

2. Make the blue cheese by mashing the cheese with the Greek yogurt before adding in some white vinegar and lemon juice. Refrigerate till ready to serve.

3. Bring the air fryer to a temperature of 204°C/400°F.

4. Cooking in batches, carefully arrange the chicken wing pieces in the basket and allow cooking for 22 minutes. Remember to flip halfway through. Cook till nice crispy and cooked through.

5. Once cooked, serve and top with the rest of the hot sauce. Put some celery, carrots, and the refrigerated blue cheese dip on the side.

AIR FRYER CAULIFLOWER

Time: 20 minutes | Servings 4

Kcal 45, Carbs 8g/0.28oz, Fats 1g/0.03oz, Proteins 3g/0.11oz, Fiber 2g/0.07oz

INGREDIENTS

- A pinch of salt
- 2g/½ a teaspoon of garlic powder
- 1 egg white
- 500g/4 cups of cauliflower florets
- 23g/¼ cup of panko breadcrumbs

PREPARATION

1. Bring the air fryer to a temperature of 200°C/390°F.
2. In a bowl, put the cauliflower florets and mix with the egg white making sure each floret is coated.
3. Now add some salt and garlic powder and toss well for even distribution.
4. Pour in the panko breadcrumbs and mix up everything.
5. Put the cauliflower in the fryer basket and allow cooking for 10 minutes before drawing and tossing the basket.
6. Cook for an additional 5 minutes till cooked to your liking.

AIR FRYER SOUTHWEST EGG ROLLS

Time: 20 minutes | Servings 12
Kcal 221, Carbs 14g/0.49oz, Fats 11g/0.39oz,
Proteins 16g/0.56oz, Fiber 2g/0.07oz

INGREDIENTS

- 250g/2 cups of shredded chicken
- 4g/1 teaspoon of paprika
- A pinch of salt
- 128g/1 cup of black beans
- 32g/¼ a cup of chopped green onions
- 128g/1 cup of corn kernels
- 380g/3 cups of shredded Monterey jack cheese
- 4g/1 teaspoon of mild cheese powder
- 2g/½ a teaspoon of ground cumin
- 32g/¼ cup of diced jalapeno pepper
- 64g/½ cup of finely diced red onion pepper
- 15ml/1 tablespoon water
- 12 egg roll wrappers
- 1 egg
- Veggie oil

PREPARATION

1. Mix black beans, jalapenos, bell pepper, chicken, green onion, corn, cheese, and some seasoning and set aside.
2. Crack and mix the egg with some water before whisking.
3. Scoop approximately ½ a cup of the chicken mixture on a wrapper. Lightly apply some egg wash on the outer side of the wrapper before folding the two-sided of the egg wrapper almost touching.
4. Fold the top part and tightly roll the egg roll to a tight fold then place it on a parchment paper.
5. Lightly coat each egg roll with vegetable oil before cooking in the fryer for 5 minutes under a temperature of 190°C/375°F.
6. Flip each roll using tongs and fry for another 5 minutes more or till the exterior gets nice and crispy.
7. Serve warm with a sauce of your choice.

AIR FRYER FRIED RICE

Time: 20 minutes | Servings 4
Kcal 618, Carbs 121g/4.3oz, Fats 7g/0.25oz, Proteins 14g/0.49oz, Fiber 4g/0.14oz

INGREDIENTS

- 2 scrambled eggs
- 380g/3 cups of cooked cold rice
- 128g/1 cup of frozen cauliflower and carrots
- 15ml/1 tablespoon of veggie oil
- 42g/⅓ cup of coconut aminos

PREPARATION

1. In a deep bowl, mix in the cold cooked rice and frozen veggies.
2. Add in the scrambled eggs and mix further.
3. Now put in the coconut aminos and veggie oil and mix.
4. Transfer the mixture into an oven-safe container.
5. Air fry for 15 minutes under a temperature of 190°C/375°F.
6. Stir the bucket after every 5 minutes to ensure even cooking.
7. Serve and enjoy.

AIR FRYER CHICKEN PARMESAN

Time: 20 minutes | Servings 4
Kcal 375, Carbs 18.9g/0.67oz, Fats 16.1g/15.7oz,
Proteins 38.6g/1.36oz, Fiber 1.6g/0.05oz

INGREDIENTS

- Sliced basil
- 2 large eggs
- 450g/1lb chicken breast
- 42g/⅓ cup of Italian seasoned panko
- 4g/1 teaspoon of salt
- 32g/¼ cup of whole wheat flour (white)
- 80ml/⅓ cup of marinara sauce
- 64g/½ cup of shredded mozzarella cheese
- 18g/4½ teaspoons of Italian seasoning.
- 64g/½ cup of shredded parmesan cheese
- 34g/2 tablespoons of divided parmesan cheese
- 42g/⅓ cup of Italian seasoned breadcrumbs

PREPARATION

1. Put the chicken between two parchment papers before flattening using a mallet.
2. Whisk the eggs carefully in a bowl.
3. Combine the Italian seasoning, panko, breadcrumbs, salt, and some parmesan cheese in a bigger bowl and mix thoroughly.
4. Have the flour in a different bowl.
5. Coat each piece in flour, then brush with the eggs, and finally, generously coat with the panko mixture.
6. Air fry for 10 minutes under a temperature of 204°C/400°F until crispy.
7. Remove and spread the marinara sauce before topping with the rest of the mozzarella and parmesan cheese.
8. Cook for an additional 5 minutes till the cheese is nice and melted and the chicken gets an internal temperature of 73°C/165°F.
9. Garnish with some basil and enjoy!

AIR FRYER ITALIAN PORK CHOPS

Time: 20 minutes | Servings 3
Kcal 495, Carbs 18g/0.63oz, Fats 22g/0.78oz,
Proteins 53g/1.87oz, Fiber 2g/0.07oz

INGREDIENT

- Garlic powder
- 245g/1 cup of heated marinara sauce
- Black pepper
- 3x170g/3x6oz pork chops
- Smoked paprika
- 54g/½ a cup of breadcrumbs
- 30ml/2 tablespoons of chopped Italian parsley
- 1 large egg
- 50g/½ a cup of grated parmesan cheese
- 56g/½ a cup of grated mozzarella cheese
- Cooking spray
- A pinch of salt

PREPARATION

1. Add some paprika, salt, black pepper, and garlic powder to the pork to taste.
2. and cook for another 2 minutes till melted.
3. Serve with some Crack and beat the eggs in a small bowl.
4. Mix the breadcrumbs, parsley and parmesan cheese in a separate bowl.
5. Soak each piece of pork in the egg before dredging in the breadcrumbs making sure each side is coated.
6. Spray some oil to both sides of the pork.
7. Bring the fryer to a temperature of 190°C/375°F and cook the pork for 10-12 minutes.
8. Flip the pork chops after 6 minutes and continue cooking till you get an internal temperature of 62-65°C/145-160°F or until golden brown.
9. Drizzle some cheese marinara sauce on the side.

AIR FRYER CHICKEN AND VEGETABLES

Time: 20 minutes | Servings 4
Kcal 230, Carbs 8g/0.28oz, Fats 10g/0.35oz,
Proteins 26g/0.92oz, Fiber 3g/ 0.120oz

INGREDIENTS

- 128g/1 cup of broccoli florets
- 56g/½ cup of finely chopped onions
- 1 chopped zucchini
- 450g/1lb of bite-size chicken breast pieces
- 30ml/2 tablespoons of olive oil
- 2g/½ a teaspoon of garlic powder, pepper, chili powder, and salt (each)
- 2 cloves of minced garlic
- 15ml/1 tablespoon of Italian seasoning
- 128g/1 cup of chopped bell pepper

PREPARATION

1. Bring the air fryer to a temperature of 204°C/400°F.
2. Cut the veggies into smaller pieces and combine them with the already sliced chicken breasts.
3. Season and oil then mix well.
4. For 10 minutes, air fry the mixture. Remember to toss 5 minutes into the cooking time.
5. Make sure the meat cooks well and veggies are charred to your liking.
6. Remember you may need to cook in more than 1 batch relative to the fryer size.

AIR FRYER BRUSSELS SPROUTS

Time: 22 minutes | Servings 4
Kcal 143, Carbs 14g/0.49oz, Fats 7g/0.24oz, Proteins 10g/0.35oz, Fiber 6g/0.21oz

INGREDIENTS

- 4g/1 teaspoon of garlic parsley salt
- 68g/4 tablespoons of parmesan cheese
- 900g/2lb of Brussels sprouts
- 64g/½ cup of precooked bacon
- 15ml/1 tablespoon of olive oil

PREPARATION

1. Wash and cut the Brussel sprouts into manageable bite-size pieces.
2. Add some parsley garlic salt, olive oil, and top with parmesan cheese. Mix everything up nice.
3. Cook up the veggie mixture in the air fryer over a temperature of 390°C/298°F for 12 minutes.
4. Remember to toss halfway through to get every side that crispy finish.
5. Put in the bacon and cook for an additional 5 minutes.
6. Serve and enjoy!

AIR FRYER PORK TENDERLOIN

Time: 26 minutes | Servings 4
Kcal 412, Carbs 30g/1.06oz, Fats 7g/0.25oz, Protein 28g/0.99oz., Fiber 1g/0.04oz

INGREDIENTS

- 34g/2 tablespoons of brown sugar
- 4g/1 teaspoon of ground mustard
- 1g/¼ teaspoon of garlic powder
- 800g/1¾lbs of pork tenderloin
- 4g/1 teaspoon of smoked paprika
- 4g/1 teaspoon of salt
- 2g/½ teaspoon of ground black pepper powder
- 7ml/½ tablespoon of olive oil
- 2g/½ teaspoon of onion powder
- A pinch of cayenne

PREPARATION

1. Put the dry ingredients in a bowl and mix thoroughly.
2. Remove excess fat from the loin.
3. Coat the loin with the olive oil before rubbing it with the spice mix all over till evenly coated.
4. Bring the air fryer to a temperature of 204°C/400°F for five minutes.
5. Place the loin in the fryer and allow cooking for 22 minutes till you achieve an internal temperature of 62-71°C/145°-160° F.
6. When cooked, slice into thin pieces on a chopping board and serve immediately.

CRISPY COCONUT SHRIMP

Time: 40 minutes | Servings 4
Kcal 690, Carbs 4g/0.14oz, Fats 68g/2.4oz, Protein 15g/0.53oz, Fiber 4g/0.14oz

INGREDIENTS

- 570g/1¼lb of jumbo raw shrimp
- 43g/⅓ cup of all-purpose flour
- 128g/1 cup of panko breadcrumbs
- 128g/1 cup of shredded sweetened coconut
- 2 large eggs
- A pinch of salt
- 2g/½ teaspoon of garlic powder
- 10ml/2 teaspoons of mayonnaise
- ½ squeezed lime
- 80ml/⅓ cup of sweet chili sauce

PREPARATION

1. Quickly clean and rinse the shrimp on running water before pat drying using paper towels.
2. In the first bowl, mix flour, garlic powder, and salt. Stir to combine.
3. Crack the eggs in the second bowl and whisk to combine.
4. Mix and toss the panko breadcrumbs and coconut in the last bowl.
5. Holding the shrimp by the tail, dredge in flour, then dip in the eggs, and lastly in the coconut mixture.
6. Place the shrimp on a parchment paper and do the same to the rest.
7. When you are done, refrigerate for 30 minutes.
8. Bring the air fryer to a temperature of 190°C/375°F.
9. Spray the shrimp with some coconut cooking spray before placing it in the basket.
10. Cook for 8 minutes flipping halfway through and cook until nice and crispy.
11. Combine the mayo, chili sauce, and lime juice to make the sauce. Mix thoroughly to the desired consistency.
12. Serve the shrimp with the sauce on the side.

AIR FRYER REUBEN STROMBOLI

Time: 23 minutes | Serving 6
Kcal 335, Carbs 30g/1.05oz, Fats 16g/0.56oz,
Proteins 18g/0.63oz, Fiber 2g/0.07oz

INGREDIENTS

- 340g/12oz of fresh pizza dough
- Cooking spray
- Thousand Island
- 6 Swiss cheese
- 15ml/1 tablespoon of Thousand Island dressing
- 225g/½lb of thinly sliced corn beef
- 128g/1 cup of sauerkraut
- 2g/½ teaspoon of garlic salt

PREPARATION

1. Roll the pizza dough into nice rectangles about 10 inches long then top with the Thousand Island dressing.
2. Leaving a 1-inch border, arrange in layers the corned beef, sauerkraut, and cheese.
3. Beginning from the longer end, roll the rough up stretching the ends and tucking everything under.
4. Coat with some cooking spray and carefully position the seam side down on the basket.
5. Drizzle some garlic salt over.
6. Preheat the fryer and cook the Stromboli under a temperature of 176°C/350°F for 15 minutes.
7. Serve with some Thousand Island dressing.

AIR FRYER CHURROS WITH CHOCOLATE SAUCE

Time: 85 minutes | Servings 12

Kcal 173, Carbs 12g/0.42oz, Fats 11g/0.39oz, Proteins 3g/012oz, Fiber 1g/0.03oz

INGREDIENTS

- 125ml/½ cup of water
- 2 large eggs
- 1g/¼ kosher salt
- 42g/⅓ cup of granulated sugar
- 64g/½ a cup of divided unsalted butter
- 8g/2 teaspoons of ground cinnamon
- 64g/½ a cup of all-purpose flour
- 100g/4oz of bittersweet baking chocolate
- 30ml/2 tablespoons of vanilla kefir
- 51g/3 tablespoons of heavy cream

PREPARATION

1. Over medium temperature, heat oil, water, salt and ¼ of butter in a saucepan.
2. Reduce heat to a low before adding flour and stirring thoroughly till the dough is smooth.
3. Continue stirring for around 3 minutes till the dough pulls away easily from the sides of the pan.
4. Transfer the dough to a bowl and continue stirring till slightly cooled before adding an egg at a time while stirring until smooth.
5. Transfer to a piping bag with a star tip and chill for 30 minutes.
6. Using the piping bag, make 6 x 3-inch pieces and arrange them in the basket.
7. Air fry at 193/380 for 10 minutes or till nice and golden brown.
8. Mix and stir sugar and cinnamon in a bowl. Coat the cooked churros with melted butter then roll in the cinnamon-sugar mixture.
9. Put the chocolate and cream in a microwave-ready bowl and heat until nice and melted. Add in the kefir and stir.
10. Serve the churros with chocolate sauce for dipping.

AIR FRYER CLASSIC FISH AND CHIPS

Time: 45 minutes | Serves 4

Kcal 415, Carbs 46g/1.46oz, Fats 7g/0.25oz, Proteins 44g/1.55oz, Fiber 4g/0.14oz

INGREDIENTS

- 2 large eggs
- 30ml/2 tablespoons of water
- 2280g/10oz scrubbed russet potatoes
- 4-170g/6oz skinless tilapia fillets
- 128g/1 cup of whole wheat panko
- 5g/1¼ teaspoon of divided kosher salt
- 128g/1 cup of all-purpose wheat flour
- 125ml/½ cup of malt vinegar
- Cooking spray

PREPARATION

1. Cut the potatoes into neat spirals using a spiralizer.

2. Working in batches, arrange the spirals in 1 layer then spray lightly with a coat of oil. Ensure the oil is well distributed.

3. For 10 minutes fry at 190°C/375°F or until they are crispy and golden brown. Be sure to toss 5 minutes into the cooking for that even cooking.

4. Once cooked, top with some salt to taste before covering to keep warm.

5. Put flour in a bowl and mix with ½ teaspoon of water.

6. In another separate dish, crack the eggs and whisk with water to achieve an even egg wash.

7. Mix the remainder of the salt with panko in another dish and stir gently.

8. Using a knife divide each fillet into two. Dredge each strip in the flour, before coating with the egg wash and finish off by rolling in the panko. Be sure to press using your hand for everything to stick. Spray with a coat of oil.

9. Working in batches once more, in one layer, place each fillet and air fry at 190°C/375°F. Air fry till nice and brown preferably for 20 minutes. Flip the fillets after 10 minutes.

10. Serve two fillets per plate with equal amounts of potato spirals. Be sure to accompany each plate with 2 tablespoons of malt vinegar.

AIR FRYER ROASTED SALMON WITH FENNEL SALAD

Time: 25 minutes | Servings 4

Kcal 464, Carbs 9g/0.32oz, Fats 30g/1.06oz, Proteins 38g/1.34oz, Fiber 3g/0.1oz

INGREDIENTS

- 4g/1 teaspoon of freshly chopped thyme
- 30ml/2 tablespoons of olive oil
- 8g/2 teaspoons of freshly chopped flat-leaf parsley
- 4x170g/6oz of skinless center-cut salmon fillet
- 170ml/⅔ cup of Greek yogurt
- 4g/1 teaspoon of divided kosher salt
- 500g/4 cups of thinly sliced fennel
- 34g/2 tablespoon of chopped fresh dill
- 30ml/2 tablespoon of fresh orange juice
- 1 grated clove of garlic
- 15ml/1 teaspoon of fresh lemon juice

PREPARATION

1. Bring the oven to a temperature of 93°C/200°F.
2. Combine and mix parsley, thyme, and a pinch of salt.
3. Brush the salmon pieces with oil before coating with the herb mixture evenly.
4. Put two pieces of salmon in the fryer and cook at 176°C/350°F till the desired finish.
5. Cook preferably for 10 minutes flipping the fillets halfway through.
6. Transfer the fillets to the oven to keep warm.
7. Repeat for the rest of the fillets.
8. As the fillets warm, combine yogurt, garlic, lemon juice, orange juice, salt, fennel, and dill in a bowl and mix well.
9. Serve the fillets over the salad.

VEGGIE QUESADILLAS

Time: 40 minutes | Serves 4
Kcal 291, Carbs 36g/1.23oz, Proteins 17g/0.6oz, Fats 8g/0.28oz, Fiber 8g/0.28oz

INGREDIENTS

- 128g/1 cup of sliced red bell pepper
- Cooking spray
- 120g/4 ounces of reduced shredded cheddar cheese
- 57g/2oz of reduced-fat Greed yogurt.
- 4 6-inch sprouted whole grain flour tortilla
- 128g/1 cup of sliced zucchini
- 128g/1 cup of unsalted black beans.
- 34g/2 tablespoons of chopped cilantro
- 15ml/1 tablespoon fresh lime juice
- 5ml/1 teaspoon lime zest
- 1g/¼ ground cumin
- 64g/½ a cup of drained refrigerated Pico de Gallo

PREPARATION

1. Spread the tortilla on a working surface and add on one half of the tortilla sprinkle some cheese.
2. Top the cheese, zucchini slices, black beans, and ¼ cup of red bell pepper slices on each tortilla.
3. Finish off with the remaining shredded cheddar cheese.
4. Fold the other half to form half-moon shaped tortilla quesadillas.
5. Gently spray the quesadillas with oil and secure with toothpicks.
6. Coat the basket with a light oil spray and put it in 2 quesadillas.
7. Air fry at 204°C/400°F for 10 minutes till the veggies soften, cheese melts, and the quesadillas turn golden brown.
8. In a different bowl combine cumin, zest, and lime juice.
9. Slice the quesadillas in wedges and garnish with some cilantro. Be sure to serve each quesadilla with some cumin cream and a generous amount of Pico de Gallo.

SNACKS

AIR FRYER CHICKPEAS

Time: 20 minutes | Serving 4

Kcal 251, Carbs 36g/1.27oz, Proteins 11g/0.39oz, Fats 6g/0.21oz, Fiber 10g/0.3oz

INGREDIENTS

- 15ml/1 tablespoon of olive oil
- A pinch of salt
- 2g/½ a teaspoon of paprika
- 1g/¼ teaspoon of garlic powder
- 540g/19oz chickpeas can
- 1g/¼ teaspoon of onion powder
- 1g/½ teaspoon of cayenne

PREPARATION

1. Bring the air fryer to a temperature of 390°C/298°F.
2. If necessary, drain and rinse the chickpeas before mixing with the spices.
3. Air fry all the chickpeas for 15 minutes and toss the basket after 5 minutes.
4. Add some salt and pepper to taste immediately they are done.
5. Keep in an open container ready for snacking.
6. Enjoy!

CRISPY BAKED ZUCCHINI FRIES

Time: 40 minutes | Serves 6
Kcal 138, Carbs 17g/0.6oz, Fats 4g/0.14oz, Proteins 8g/0.28oz, Fiber 2g/0.07oz

INGREDIENTS

- 2 beaten eggs
- 128g/1 cup of seasoned panko breadcrumbs
- 2 medium zucchini sliced into 2-inch matchsticks
- 2g/½ teaspoon of garlic powder
- 64g/½ a cup of freshly grated parmesan cheese
- 64g/½ cup of white whole purpose flour
- 2g/½ teaspoon of salt

PREPARATION

1. Bring the oven to a temperature of 218°C/425°F.
2. Line the baking sheet with parchment paper and put it aside.
3. Pour the beaten eggs in one bowl and flour in another separate bowl.
4. Mix the panko breadcrumbs with salt and garlic in another separate bowl.
5. Roll the zucchini slices in the bowl with the flour, then dip in the egg bowl, and finally roll in the breadcrumbs mixture and ensure even coating.
6. Working in batches, arrange 8 fries in the baking sheet.
7. Cook till the crumbs turn brown or for 10 minutes depending on how much zucchini you put in the fryer.
8. Serve and enjoy!

AIR FRYER MOZZARELLA BALLS

Time: 90minutes | Servings 12
Kcal 206, Carbs 627.3mg/0.02oz, Fats 9.1g/0.32oz,
Proteins 13.3g/0.47oz, Fiber5.2g/0.18oz

INGREDIENTS

- 1 egg
- 128g/1 cup of Italian preseasoned breadcrumbs
- 25g/1½ tablespoon of parmesan
- 17g/1 tablespoon of oregano
- 12g/3 teaspoons of corn starch
- 256g/2 cups of freshly grated mozzarella
- A pinch of salt
- 6g/1½ teaspoon of garlic powder

PREPARATION

1. Bring the air fryer to a temperature of 204°C/400°F then line the bottom of the baking sheet with a parchment paper.
2. Add the mozzarella in a bowl and combine with parmesan and cornstarch then mix thoroughly.
3. Scoop small portions of the cheese and roll into bite-size balls before freezing for 45-60 minutes.
4. Crack the egg and whisk in a small bowl.
5. Mix the breadcrumbs, garlic powder, and salt in another bowl till even.
6. Dip the cheese balls in the egg before dredging in the breadcrumbs mixture and arranging them on the baking sheet.
7. Freeze for an additional 20 minutes.
8. Once more repeat the egg, and breadcrumb process and put in the fryer basket.
9. Air fry for 20 minutes tossing the basket after every 5 minutes.
10. Transfer to a baking sheet just before they start melting and allow cooling.
11. Serve with a sauce of your choice.

AIR FRYER KETO JALAPENO POPPERS

Time: 15 minutes | Servings 4

Kcal 281, Carbs 2g/0.07oz, Fats 29g/1oz, Protein 4g/0.14oz, Fiber 4g/0.14oz

INGREDIENTS

- 110g/4oz goat cheese
- Medium onion
- Cilantro
- A pinch of salt
- 4g/1 teaspoon of chili powder
- 2g/½ teaspoon of garlic powder
- Crushed red pepper
- 5 medium Jalapenos

PREPARATION

1. Slice the jalapenos into half then remove the seeds.
2. Mix the spices thoroughly.
3. Add the spice blend to the goat cheese and mix carefully with a fork.
4. Scoop the goat cheese mixture and spread on the halved Jalapenos before putting them in the air fryer.
5. Fry under a temperature of 176°C/350°F.
6. Depending on the desired finish, cook for 8 minutes for that soft pepper or cook 5 minutes more for a nice crispy finish.

AIR FRYER PARMESAN POTATOES

Time: 20 minutes | Servings 1

Kcal 178, Carbs 24g/0.85oz, Fats 6g/0.21oz, Proteins 7g/0.25oz, Fiber 3g/0.09oz

INGREDIENTS

- 30ml/2 tablespoon of olive oil
- 4g/1 teaspoon of dry Italian seasoning
- 2g/½ a teaspoon of salt
- 64g/½ cup of shredded parmesan
- 450g/1lb of small-sized baby potatoes

PREPARATION

1. Gently coat the basket with nonstick oil.
2. Bring the fryer to a temperature of 187°C/370°F for 5 minutes.
3. Combine the potatoes, Italian seasoning, oil, salt, and cheese in a bowl.
4. Use your hands to mix everything up.
5. Put the mixture in the air fryer.
6. Judging from the potato sizes, fry for 15-20 minutes.
7. Remember to toss the basket every 5 minutes.
8. Serve and enjoy!

AIR FRY CORN TORTILLA CHIPS

Time: 4 minutes | Servings 1
Kcal 133, Carbs 13g/0.46oz, Fats, 4g/0.13oz, Proteins 5g/0.16oz, Fiber 1g/0.03oz

INGREDIENTS

- A pinch of salt
- 8 corn tortillas
- 15ml/1 tablespoon of olive oil

PREPARATION

1. Bring the Air fryer to a temperature of 200°C/392°F.
2. Cut the tortillas into triangles using a knife.
3. Gently coat each piece with olive oil.
4. Place half of the oil-coated tortillas in the basket and air fry for 3 minutes.
5. Repeat with the second batch and remember to shake halfway through.
6. Add some salt to taste then serve.

LOW CARB AIR FRYER PICKLES

Time: 35 minutes | Servings 7
Kcal 210, Carbs 8g/0.28oz, Fats 17.6g/0.62oz,
Proteins 7.5g/0.26oz, Fiber 1.7g/0.06oz

INGREDIENTS

- 96g/¾ cup heavy whipping cream
- Ranch dressing
- 35 dill slices of pickle
- 64g/½ cup of almond flour
- 1 egg
- 34g/2 tablespoons of freeze-dried dill
- 1g/¼ teaspoon of paprika
- Sriracha Mayonnaise
- 1g/¼ teaspoon of cayenne pepper
- 56g/2oz of pork rinds
- 8g/2 teaspoons of black pepper

PREPARATION

1. Crack and beat an egg in a bowl. Add on the whipping cream and cayenne then mix thoroughly.
2. Shred the pork rinds in a food processor till they become crumbs.
3. Transfer half of the shredded pork rinds in a bowl.
4. Mix the remainder of the pork rinds with dill, paprika, almond flour, and black pepper in a different bowl.
5. Dip each piece of pickle in the plain rinds, then the eggs mix, and finally the almond flour mix.
6. Cooking in batches, layer the pickles on the basket and air fry under a temperature of 390°C/298°F or till nice and brown.
7. Serve the pickles with Sriracha Mayonnaise and Ranch dressing.

AIR FRIED POTATO CHIPS

Time: | Servings 4
Kcal 74.3, Carbs 17.6g/0.62oz, Fats 0g, Proteins 2g/0.07oz, Fiber 1.4g/0.05oz

INGREDIENTS

- Thinly sliced Russet potato
- 400g/14oz of grapeseed oil cooking spray
- Sea salt

PREPARATION

1. Squeeze out the moisture from potatoes using paper towels.
2. Coat the basket with some oil before arranging the potato pieces. Do so in batches.
3. Coat the top of the potatoes with oil before adding some salt.
4. Air fry the potato slices under a temperature of 232°C/450°F for 15 minutes till the edges turn brown and crispy. Depending on the thickness of the slices adjust the cooking time accordingly.
5. Once cooked, remove and let them crisp up in open air overnight.

AIR FRYER ONION RINGS

Time: 22 minutes | Servings 2

Kcal 193, Carbs 26g/0.92oz, Fats 8g/0.28oz, Proteins 4g/0.14oz, Fiber 2g/0.07oz

INGREDIENTS

- 128g/1 cup of panko breadcrumbs
- 30ml/2 teaspoons of olive oil
- 1 yellow onion sliced into thin rings
- 64g/½ a cup of wheat flour
- 1 egg
- 4g/1 teaspoon of paprika
- Oil spray
- 4g/1 teaspoon of divided salt
- 124ml/½ cup of buttermilk

PREPARATION

1. Combine paprika, flour, and ½ teaspoon of salt in one bowl and mix.
2. In another bowl, combine and mix ¼ of the flour mix from the first bowl, buttermilk, and the egg to form a paste.
3. In the third bowl, combine the breadcrumbs with the remainder of the salt, and olive oil thoroughly until even.
4. Divide the breadcrumb mixture into two and pour in a separate bowl to switch when one gets too sticky.
5. Now dip the onion rings in the flour, buttermilk mixture then in the breadcrumbs.
6. Spray the basket with some oil before carefully arranging the rings with enough space between them. You could also put smaller rings inside bigger rings but ensure there is a separation between them.
7. Cook at 204°C/400°F for 15 minutes till golden fry.
8. Halfway through, spray with some oil before flipping the rings to the other side.
9. Serve when both sides are cooked.

AIR FRIED SWEET POTATO

Time: 35 minutes | Serves 3
Kcal 153, Carbs 26g/0.92oz, Fats 4g/0.14oz, Proteins 2g/0.07oz, Fiber 3g/0.12oz

INGREDIENTS

- 34g/2 tablespoons of kosher salt
- 15ml/1 tablespoon of olive oil
- 3 sweet potatoes

PREPARATION

1. Carefully wash your sweet potatoes in running water before creating air holes using a fork.
2. Drizzle some olive oil and salt then coat evenly using your hands.
3. Place the coated sweet potatoes in the basket.
4. Air fry at 390°F/298°C for 30-40 minutes till nice and tender in the insides.
5. Serve with a topping of your choice.

SPECIAL AIR FRYER DESSERT RECIPES

AIR FRYER CINNAMON ROLLS

Time: 30 minutes | Servings 6
Kcal 505, Carbs 2g/0.07oz, Fats 49g/1.73oz,
Proteins 12g/1.42oz, Fibers 1g/0.04oz

INGREDIENTS

- Kosher salt
- 30ml/2 tablespoons melted butter
- 2g/½ teaspoon of ground cinnamon
- All-purpose flour
- 40g/⅓ cup of brown sugar
- 230g/8oz refrigerated crescent rolls
- 15ml/1 teaspoon of whole milk
- 60g/2oz softened cream cheese
- 64g/½ cup of powdered sugar

PREPARATION

1. Butter the parchment paper and line it at the base of the basket.
2. In a bowl, mix brown sugar, butter, a pinch of salt and cinnamon. Mix till fluffy and smooth.
3. Flour the working surface and spread out the rolls into a flat piece.
4. Holding by the seams, fold into half then roll into a 9 by 7-inch rectangle.
5. Cover the dough with the butter mixture leaving a 1-inch border around.
6. Beginning from one edge, roll the dough in a jelly roll like fashion before cutting crosswise into 6 equal pieces.
7. Carefully place the rolls in the air fryer keeping the cut side up and be sure to give each roll enough space.
8. Cook the rolls at 176°C/350°F for 10 minutes or until they turn golden brown.
9. In a separate bowl, stir together cream cheese, powdered sugar, and milk into a thin uniform glaze.
10. Serve the cinnamon rolls with a drizzle of the glaze.

AIR FRYER S'MORES

Time: 10 minutes | Servings 4
Kcal 127, Carbs 9g/0.31oz, Fats 3g/0.12oz, Proteins 5g/0.17oz, Fiber 1g/0.03oz

INGREDIENTS

- 4 whole graham crackers
- 4 pieces of chocolate
- 2 marshmallows

PREPARATION

1. Half all the graham crackers into 8 pieces.
2. Using a pair of scissors, cut the marshmallows into halves.
3. Put the cut phase down on 4 graham pieces.
4. Place the marshmallow side up in the basket then cook for 5 minutes at a temperature of 390°C/298°F.
5. Once cooked, layer a chocolate piece on top of the graham and stack on the marshmallow top before serving.

AIR FRYER KEY LIME CUPCAKES

Time: 30 minutes | Servings 6

Kcal 218, Carbs 13g/0.45oz, Fats 14g/0.49oz, Proteins 9g/0.32oz, Fiber 0g

INGREDIENTS

- 250g/1 cup Greek yogurt
- 2 large eggs
- 5ml/1 teaspoon of vanilla essence
- 1 egg yolk
- 200g/7oz of soft cheese
- 2 limes
- 32g/¼ cup of castor sugar

PREPARATION

1. Using a hand mixture, thoroughly mix the Greek yogurt and soft cheese till nice and soft.
2. Add in the beaten eggs before mixing once more.
3. Add the vanilla essence, limes, and sugar to the same mixture and mix again.
4. Fill the contents of the mixture to 6 cupcake cases and set the remainder aside.
5. Arrange the filled up cupcake cases in the basket and cook for 10 minutes at 160°C/320°F. Fry further for 10 minutes at 180°C/356°F.
6. Transfer the remainder of the mixture into a cupcake nozzle and refrigerate for 10 minutes.
7. Remove the cupcakes from the fryer then allow 10 minutes of cooling.
8. Use the nozzle to create the top layer of your cupcake then refrigerate the cupcakes allowing the topping to set for 4 hours.

AIR FRYER BLUEBERRY HAND PIE

Time: 27 minutes | Servings 8

Kcal 251, Carbs 30g/1.06oz, Fats 12g/0.42oz, Proteins 3g/0.12oz, Fiber 1g/0.03oz

INGREDIENTS

- 5ml/1 teaspoon lime juice
- 128g/1 cup of blueberries
- A pinch of salt
- 32g/2½ tablespoons of castor sugar
- Vanilla sugar
- Water
- 320g/14oz of refrigerated pie crust

PREPARATION

1. Combine sugar, blueberries, lime juice, and salt in a bowl and mix.
2. Spread out the pie crust on a working surface and cut 8 4-inch circles.
3. Put 17ml/1 tablespoon of the mixture made in one half of the circle.
4. Using water, moisten the edges of the dough and roll the empty half over the blueberry mixture.
5. Crimp the edges of the crust using a fork then make three slits on the top of the pie.
6. Spray the crust with oil then sprinkle generous amounts of vanilla sugar.
7. Bring the air fryer to a temperature of 176°C/350°F.
8. Carefully arrange 4 hand pies at a time in a single layer in the basket.
9. Air fry for 10-12 minutes till golden brown.
10. Allow cooling before serving.

FRIED BANANA S'MORES

Time: 16 minutes | 4 servings

Kcal 380, Carbs 64g/2.26oz, Fats 12g/0.42oz, Proteins 7g/0.25oz, Fiber 5g/0.18oz

INGREDIENTS

- 51g/3 tablespoons of mini chocolate chip
- 4 bananas
- 51g/3 tablespoons of mini peanut butter chips
- 51g/3 tablespoons of graham cracker cereal
- 51g/3 tablespoons of mini marshmallows

PREPARATION

1. Bring the air fryer to a temperature of 204°C/400°F.

2. Cut along the inside curve of the unpeeled banana. Be sure not to cut through the bottom peel then open to create a pocket.

3. Into each pocket, add in the marshmallows, chocolate chip, and peanut butter chips to fill in space. Force the graham cracker piece into the filling too.

4. Carefully place the bananas in the basket balancing against each other to keep that upright position with the fillings on top and out in the air.

5. Cook for 6 minutes till the bananas get soft, the chocolate chips and marshmallow have melted and toasted well. The peel should have blackened by his time.

6. Allow cooling then serve.

7. Use a spoon to scoop the filling.

AIR FRYER CHOCOLATE CAKE

Time: 35 minutes | Servings 4
Kcal 573, Carbs 253g/8.9oz, Fats 134g/4.72oz,
Proteins 43g/1.45oz, Fibers 3g/0.12oz

INGREDIENTS

- 128g/1 cup of flour
- 4g/1 teaspoon baking powder
- 10ml/2 teaspoons of vanilla
- 3 eggs
- 85g/⅔ cup of cup sugar
- 1 stick of butter
- 43g/⅓ cup of cocoa powder
- 2g/½ teaspoon of baking soda
- 125ml/½ a cup of sour cream

PREPARATION

1. Bring the air fryer to a temperature of 160°C/320°F.
2. Mix all the ingredients carefully before pouring into the oven attachment.
3. Put the attachment into the air fryer and bake for 25 minutes.
4. Check with a toothpick if the cake is ready.
5. The cake should spring back when touched, if it doesn't, continue cooking till ready.
6. Allow cooling before topping with your favorite cream.

AIR FRYER CHOCOLATE CHIP COOKIE

Time: 25 minutes | Servings 8
Kcal 1189, Carbs 176g/6.2oz, Fats 49g/1.73oz,
Proteins 13g/0.46oz, Fiber 3g/0.12oz

INGREDIENTS

- 64g/½ cup of sugar
- 1 egg
- 5ml/1 teaspoon of vanilla
- 1g/¼ teaspoon of salt
- 128g/1 cup of chocolate chips
- 125ml/½ cup of softened butter
- 64g/½ cup of light brown sugar
- 2g/½ a teaspoon of baking soda
- 290g/1½ cups of all-purpose flour

PREPARATION

1. Bring the air fryer to a temperature of 176°C/350°.
2. Grease a metal or glass pan in preparation for frying.
3. Mix butter, brown sugar, and sugar. Pour in the eggs and vanilla to the mixture and stir.
4. Add in the flour, salt, and baking soda before finishing off with the chocolate chips.
5. Be sure to stir into a nice soft dough.
6. Put the dough in the pan and bake for 10-12 minutes till brown around the edges.

AIR FRIED VEGAN BEIGNETS

Time: 90 minutes | Servings 6
Kcal 102, Carbs 15g/0.53oz, Fats 3g/0.12oz, Proteins 3g/0.12oz, Fiber 1g/0.03oz

INGREDIENTS

- 4g/1 teaspoon of organic corn starch
- 128g/1 cup of whole earth sweetener baking blend
- 6g/1½ teaspoons of active baking yeast
- 250ml/1 cup of full-fat coconut milk
- 51g/3 tablespoons of the powdered baking blend
- 10ml/2 teaspoons of vanilla
- 30ml/2 tablespoons of melted coconut oil
- 20ml/2 tablespoons of aquafaba
- 384g/3 cups of unbleached white flour

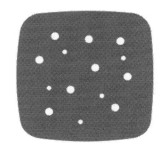

PREPARATION

1. Put the whole earth sweetener and corn starch into a blender and blend till smooth.
2. Heat the coconut milk till warm enough that you can dip in a finger.
3. Pour the warm coconut milk to the mixer together with sugar and yeast and allow to settle for 10 minutes.
4. Now mix aquafaba, coconut oil, and vanilla well before adding in flour a cup after another. Mix the dough thoroughly until it easily comes off the sides of the mixture.
5. Continue kneading for 3 minutes. The dough should be wet but easy to scrape off without sticking in your hands.
6. Transfer the dough in a mixing bowl and cover it with paper towels. Allow sitting for 1 hour to set and rise.
7. On a working surface, sprinkle some flour, spread out the dough before cutting the dough into 24 squares with a thickness of around ⅓ of an inch.
8. Let them proof for 30 minutes before cooking.
9. Bring the air fryer to a temperature of 200°C/ 390°F.
10. Working in batches, cook the beignets for 3 minutes before flipping the other side and cooking for some 2 more minutes or till nice and golden brown.
11. Once cooked sprinkle with baking blend and enjoy.

AIR BAKED MOLTEN LAVA CAKES

Time: 20 minutes | Servings 4
Kcal 473, Carbs 153g/5.4oz, Fats 64g/2.26oz,
Proteins 43g/1.45oz, Fibers 3g/0.12oz

INGREDIENTS

- 85g/3oz of unsalted butter
- 25g/1½ tablespoons of self-rising flour
- 2 eggs
- 60g/3½ tablespoon of baker's sugar
- 100g/3½ oz of dark chocolate pieces

PREPARATION

1. Grease the insides of 4 oven-ready ramekins.
2. In a microwave, melt butter, and the chocolate for 3 minutes stirring regularly.
3. Once melted, remove from the microwave and continue stirring some more.
4. Beat the eggs in a bowl then add sugar and mix well.
5. Empty the chocolate mixture into the egg mixture and stir in flour. Mix everything up till even.
6. Preheat the air fryer for 10 minutes to a temperature of 190°C/375°F.
7. Fill the ramekins to ¾ full with the flour mixture and air fry for 10 minutes.
8. Take out of the fryer and allow cooling for 2 minutes in the ramekins.
9. Flop the ramekins into a flat serving plate and gently shake to release the cake.
10. The center should be nice and gooey.
11. Enjoy with a drizzle of your choice.

AIR FRYER FRIED OREOS

Time: 14 minutes | Servings 9
Kcal 67, Carbs 10g/0.3oz, Fats 3g/0.12oz, Proteins 1g/0.03oz, Fiber 1g/0.03oz

INGREDIENTS

- Crescent sheet roll
- 9 cookies (Oreo)

PREPARATION

1. Spread the crescent sheet on a working surface.
2. Make 9 even squares with a knife.
3. Carefully wrap each cookie with the square crescent sheet.
4. Bring the air fryer to a temperature of 176°C/350°.
5. Arrange the wrapped cookies in one layer in the air fryer.
6. Be sure to shake and flop the basket halfway through.
7. Enjoy with cinnamon sprinkles.

AIR FRYER BROWNIES

Time 20 minutes | Servings 4
Kcal 385, Carbs 54g/1.9oz, Fats 18g/0.63oz, Proteins 6g/0.21oz, Fiber3g/0.12oz

INGREDIENTS

- 2 large eggs
- 15ml/1 tablespoon vegetable oil
- A pinch of salt
- 96g/¾ cup of sugar
- 64g/½ a cup all-purpose flour
- 32g/¼ cup of unsweetened cocoa powder
- 32g/¼ a cup of unsalted butter
- 1g/¼ teaspoon of baking powder
- 3ml/½ a teaspoon of vanilla extract

PREPARATION

1. Grease the insides of the baking pan whether either metallic or glass.
2. Bring the air fryer to a temperature of 165°C/330°F and let it run for 5 minutes.
3. Combine flour, vanilla extract, salt, baking powder, cocoa powder, butter, sugar, eggs, and vegetable oil, in a deep bowl then stir thoroughly.
4. Pour in the baking pan and make the top smooth.
5. Bake in the air fryer for 15 minutes checking with a toothpick. The toothpick should slide out clean when ready.
6. Once ready, allow cooling in the pan before slicing and serving.

AIR FRYER CRUSTLESS CHEESECAKE

Time: 10 minutes | Serves 2

Kcal 373, Carbs 153g/5.4oz, Fats 32g/1.13oz, Proteins 43g/1.45oz, Fibers 0g

INGREDIENTS

- 2 eggs
- 5ml/1 teaspoon lemon juice
- 96g/¾ cup of zero-calorie sugar
- 5ml/1 teaspoon vanilla extract
- 30ml/2 tablespoons of sour cream
- 450g/16oz of softened cream cheese

PREPARATIONS

1. Bring the air fryer to a temperature of 176°C/350°F.
2. Use a blender to blend and mix all the ingredients until even and lump-free. The longer you blend the silkier it gets.
3. Empty the batter into a baking pan and for 10 minutes, bake till everything sets.
4. Once cooked, allow cooling before refrigerating overnight then serve.

Printed in Great Britain
by Amazon

54569402R00066